sighting apparatus for land and air targeting. The priority for development of this weapon was rated just after the 88mm Flak. The 20mm Flak 30 was ready by 1933 and exceeded the cited requirements considerably. At first the army was entrusted with anti-aircraft defense, and in 1934 it already had twelve Flak units. On April 1, 1935, according to Göring's orders, the Flak units were placed under the command of the Luftwaffe. But in 1938 the army once again was given a 20mm Flak company with twelve guns for every machine-gun battalion.

In the Spanish Civil War of 1936 the 20mm Flak 30 was used by two batteries of the *Legion Condor* and also tested successfully in ground combat.

This weapon was basically only an improved form of the 20mm MGC/30. In the Luftwaffe Service Instructions it was described as follows: It is a "fully automatic recoil self-charger with a rocker breech, which effects the loading and ignition of the cartridge as well as the removal and ejection of the empty cartridge case automatically by utilizing the pressure of the powder gas." This provided a theoretical rate of fire of 280 shots per minute. Since the magazine had to be changed after twenty shots, in practice only about 120 shots per minute could be fired. At that rate, a barrel temperature of 225 degrees Celsius was reached and the barrel had to be changed. Explosive or antipersonnel shells with or without tracers could be used, as well as blank cartridges if a blank apparatus was installed.

To attain a higher number of scores on ever-faster aircraft, the instruments also had to be improved from World War I standards. When air targets were attacked with light weapons in World War I, the distances were only estimated with an annular foresight. Even with the inverted-image range finder later taken over from the field artillery, unsatisfactory results were attained. Finally the stereoscopic range finder already used by the navy was introduced. This instrument, of course, requires that the rangetaker can see stereoscopically, that is, three-dimensionally.

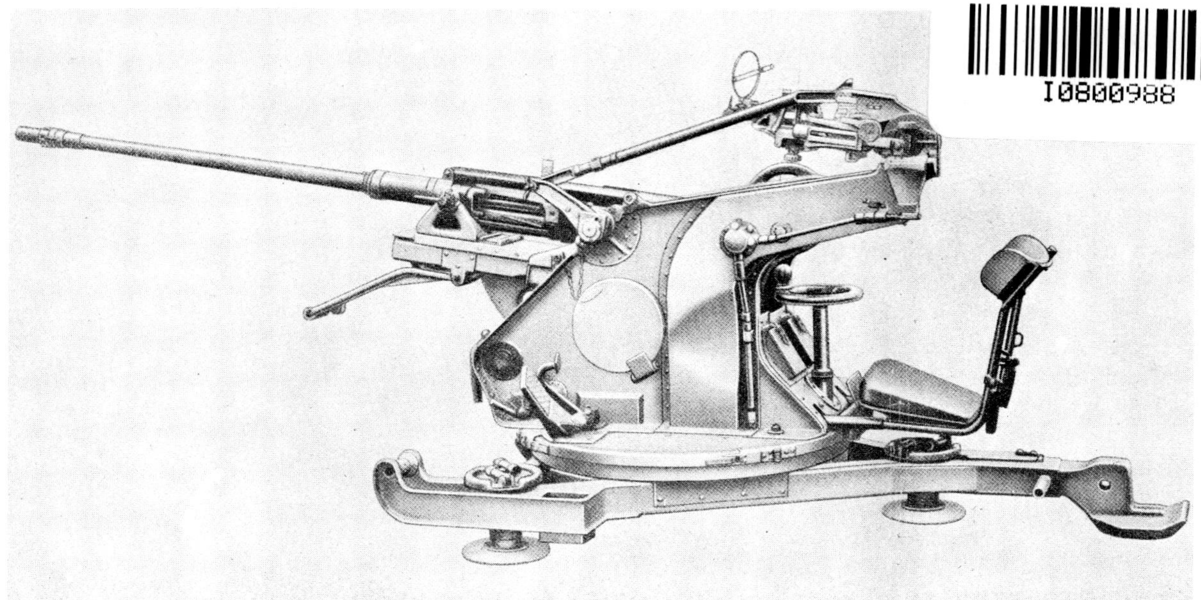

20mm Flak 30 mount with 20mm Flak 30 gun and linear sight 21 in firing position at a barrel elevation of about 20 degrees (seen from left).

Below: Crew of a 20mm Flak 30 removing Special Trailer 51 for "positioning on a foundation."

In stereoscopic range-finding, a three-dimensional picture of the target is compared with a second three-dimensional picture of a measuring system. The numbers appear in space and state the distance in hectometers. The rangetaker must coordinate the goal sighted by the device with the numbers, read them off and call them to the gun crew.

Since World War I, though, there have been not only improvements in range finders, but also constant improvements in sights, from the annular to the pivoted ring sight to the linear to Flak Sight 35 — all of which were used in World War II. For direct aim against fixed and moving land and sea targets, there was also a land-target sight. The particular difficulties involved in fighting an air target that moves in three-dimensional space demanded constant improvements to aiming devices.

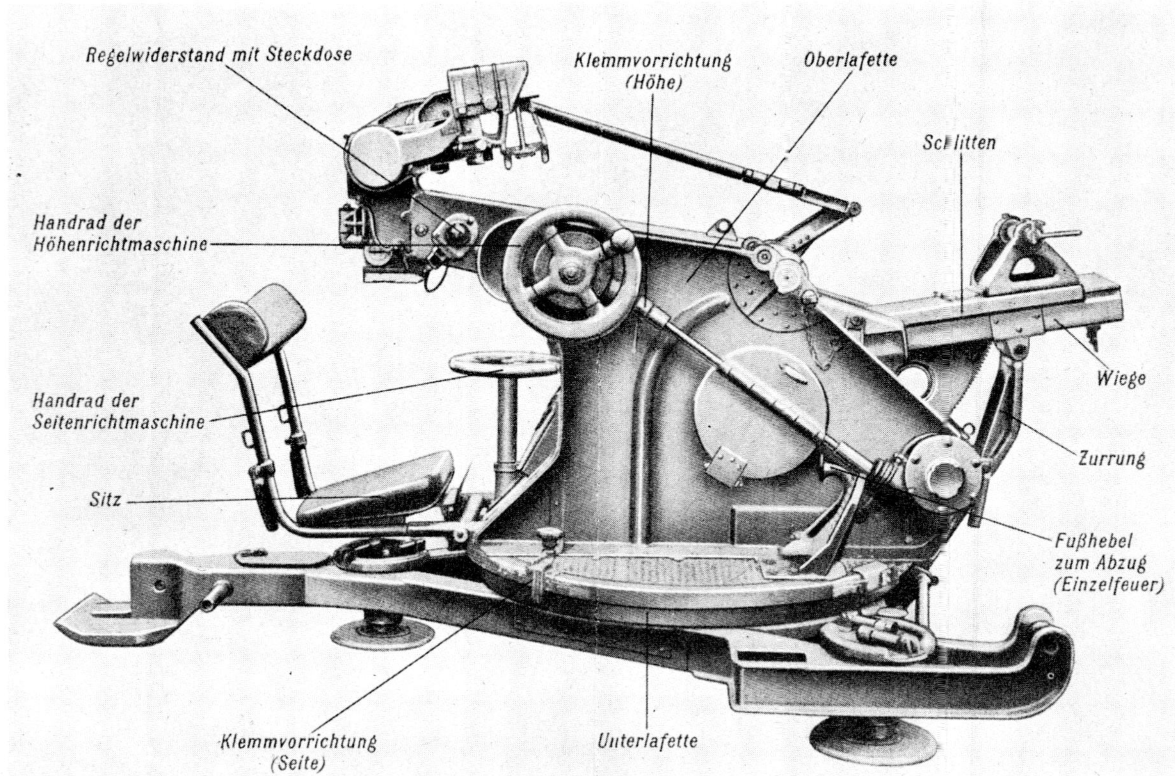

Above: The picture shows a 20mm Flak 30 mount without a gun but with the Flak Sight 30. The cradle and upper mount are locked, the view is from the right. Of the triangle attachment of the lower mount, one of the two carrying arms with adjustable horizontation can be seen at right, and at left the box for attaching the mount to Special Trailer 51. The upper mount rests on a bottom plate with a circular track and cover plate. With the foot pedal visible here near the footrest, single fire is triggered. The foot pedal to trigger sustained fire is at the left side of the 20mm Flak 30 mount. Two handwheels, one each for the elevation and traverse gears, can be seen, as can the carrier arm with the Flak Sight 35 and its control arm. The cradle serves as a guiding rail for the weapon's sled as well as to hold the brake cylinder and to elevate the weapon; it can be seen on the geared arc.

Right: Inspection of a 20mm Flak 30 gun crew.

GERMAN MEDIUM FLAK

IN COMBAT

20mm-88mm FLAK

Self-Propelled Flak
Möbelwagen
Wirbelwind
Ostwind
Kugelblitz

Werner Müller

SCHIFFER MILITARY HISTORY
West Chester, PA

Sources:

Texts:
Engelmann-Scheibert, *Deutsche Artillerie 1934-1945*
H.A. Koch, Flak
O.W. von Renz, *Deutsche Flugabwehr im 20. Jahrhundert*
Several LDv

Photos:
Federal Archives, Koblenz (BA)
Podzun-Pallas Publishing Archives
Several LDv
Horst Scheibert Archives
Schroeder Archives
Max Wüst Archives
Suhany Archives
Bibliothek für Zeitgeschichte

Translated from the German by Dr. Edward Force,
Central Connecticut State University.

Library of Congress Catalog Number: 91-62749.

Printed in the United States of America.
ISBN: 0-88740-351-4

This title was originally published under the title,
Flak auf dem Gefechtsfeld,
by Podzun-Pallas Verlag, Friedberg.

Published by Schiffer Publishing, Ltd.
1469 Morstein Road
West Chester, Pennsylvania 19380
Please write for a free catalog.
This book may be purchased from the publisher.
Please include $2.00 postage.
Try your bookstore first.

20mm quadruple Flak 38 firing at the enemy.

Foreword

Since the 20mm Flak gun was second only to the 88 as the most frequently used and thus best-known anti-aircraft gun in World War II, we decided to prepare a volume on it. In trying to include all its versions, combinations and types of use, we came upon a wealth of material that became more and more interesting — especially in the realm of "self-propelled anti-aircraft guns" in a broad sense, and even outside of this caliber.

Therefore we decided to expand this volume, originally dedicated only to the 20mm Flak gun, to include Flak guns of all calibers except armored types.

We believe that such a presentation has not been made before now, and we hope that this volume will thus be of particular interest.

Anti-aircraft guns at Narva, April 1944. German Army Flak (20mm Flak 30) fight off a Soviet bomber attack on Narva. The tree trunks in the foreground serve as makeshift shrapnel protection.

20mm Flak 30

Even during World War I, as airplanes flew higher and faster, they necessitated the development of high-performance anti-aircraft guns. But this development was interrupted by the Treaty of Versailles, since the German Reich was banned from owning any anti-aircraft (Flak) guns. Yet as of 1828 the army had a 20mm weapon, the MGC/30. Only in 1932 did the Geneva Disarmament Conference recognize Germany as having equal rights to other countries for self-defense. Immediately, on December 6, 1932, the Reichswehr Minister then in office presented a plan to establish and equip an anti-aircraft artillery, as well as the military requirements for its weapons.

According to this plan, among other things, special weapons were to be developed for use against low-level air attacks — above and beyond defense by the troops with their own weapons. These weapons had to fulfill certain prerequisites appropriate to their use. Their total weight was not to exceed 200 kg, so they could be moved quickly by men or horses as well as by trucks. Their traverse was to be 360 degrees, their elevation from -20 to +90 degrees. For this purpose the 20mm caliber appeared to be suitable, and the cartridge was to explode automatically after a certain distance, so as not to fall to earth as a whole shell. In addition, the shrapnel of the shell should be able to penetrate parts of aircraft. Also required were: A Vo (velocity of the shell when leaving the barrel) of 800 to 1000 meters per second, a range of up to 2000 meters, light tracer up to that distance, a rate of fire of 300 to 500 shots per minute, and

Above: 20mm Flak 30 mount with 20mm Flak 30 gun ready to travel on Special Trailer 51 (seen from left).

Below: 20mm Flak 30 mount with 20mm Flak 30 gun ready to travel on Special Trailer 51 (seen from right).

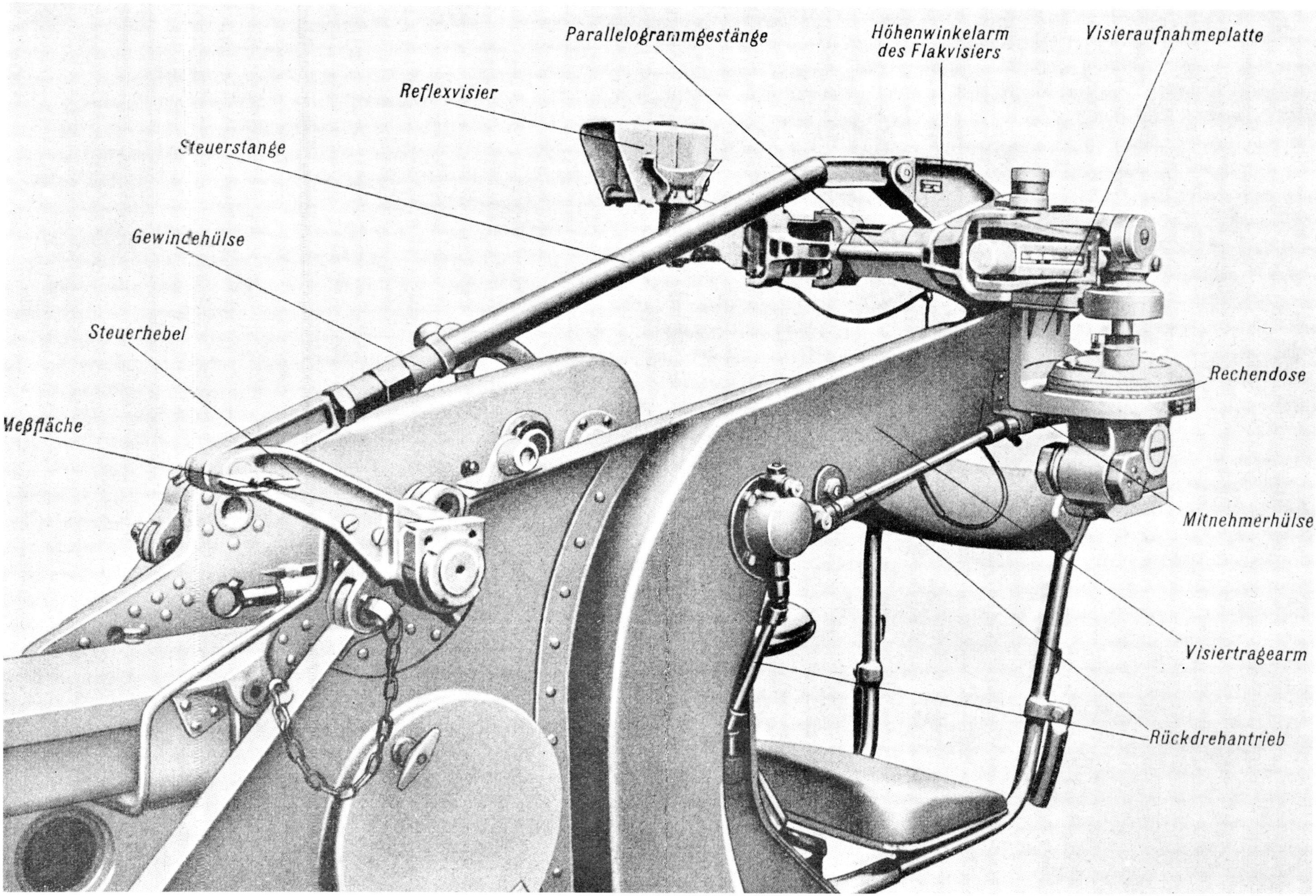

Flak Sight 35 with sight mount and control on 20mm Flak 30 mount.

Upper left: A 20mm Flak 30 in a prepared position. The boards of the breastwork are meant to prevent lowering the barrel too far. At left, the leader observes the target, while the K1 aims the gun at the target by using the Flak Sight 35.(BA)

Above: This gun stands on the flat terrain of North Africa as if on a platter. Heightened alertness is called for, so as not to be surprised by the enemy. For that reason, two crewmen are serving as aircraft spotters.(BA)

Left: 20mm Flak 30 (Army Flak) in action on land, securing the entry to a harbor.(BA)

Thus in the theory of anti-aircraft fire, the theory of firing on flying targets, one had to begin with certain prerequisites. Scores were only to be made when, during the flight time of the shell, no unexpected change in the flight direction, height or speed took place. The difficulty was the calculation of the future position of the target, which had to lie in the flight direction of flight, at the distance ahead of the target that it covered during the flight time of the shell. Even when one considered all the known components, such as gravity, air resistance, shot mass, shot diameter, air weight, rifling deviation, barrel wear, shot speed, powder composition, powder temperature, wind velocity and direction, one could predict the behavior of the target during the shot flight time only from its previous behavior in order to determine the future position. That was the point at which the weapon had to be aimed in terms of traverse, elevation and distance.

Rule of thumb: Flight speed (v) times shell flight time = distance (s)To equalize the earth's gravity and the air resistance, the angle of the barrel's elevation had to be raised by an additional angle (the angle between the shot trajectory and the extended axis of the barrel).

Upper right: A 20mm Flak 30 secures the loading of troops and most necessary materials from Courland in 1945.

Right: A 20mm Flak 20 mount with 20mm Flak 30 gun and Linear Sight 21 ready to fire at an elevation of about 70 degrees (seen from right rear).

20mm Flak 30 Technical Data

Dimensions	
Length of weapon with muzzle brake	2251 mm
Length of barrel	1300 mm
Length of barrel with muzzle brake	1450 mm
Length of cartridge bed	140.6 mm
Length of rifled area	1159.4 mm
Number of riflings	8
Depth of riflings	0.35 mm
Width of riflings	5.35 mm
Width of fields	2.5 mm
Length of rifling (constant right spiral)	720 mm

Weights	
Weight of the weapon	64.2 kg
Weight of recoiling parts	34.3 kg
Weight of barrel with muzzle brake	18.3 kg

Ballistics	
Weight of cartridge	143 g
Initial velocity (V_o)	830 m/sec
Shot range	4800 m
Altitude	3800 m
Theoretical firing speed, rounds per minute	ca. 300

Barrel heat	
60 rounds sustained fire	ca. 150 C
120 rounds in 1-2 min. (change barrel!)	ca. 250 C
120 rounds in 3-4 min. (change barrel!)	ca. 220 C
120 rounds in 7-8 min. (change barrel)	ca. 200 C

Asbestos cloths were used to hold the barrel when changing.

Aiming Capability	20mm Flak 30	20mm Flak 38
Elevation range	-10 to +90	-20 to +90
Traverse range	360 degrees	360 degrees
Elevation change per turn (fine)	407'	4 degrees
Elevation change per turn (coarse)	none	12 degrees
Traverse change per turn (fine)	none	10 degrees
Traverse change per turn (coarse)	29 deg. 21'	20 degrees
Firing Height		
Dismounted	740 mm	760 mm
On special trailer	1080 mm	1120 mm
Weights		
Mount (without weapon and sight)	364 kg	326 kg
Mount (with weapon, sight, etc.)	470 kg	412 kg
Mount in firing position with weapon, 1 or to (for 38) filled magazines, cover and equipment	770 kg	750 kg

20mm Flak 38

In 1939 the troops received an improved 20mm Flak 38. This weapon was lighter, its traverse and elevating gear had coarse and fine adjustments. Thus it could be aimed more quickly and precisely. Above all, the firing speed of a theoretical 480 rounds (= 2.5 seconds for a 20-round magazine) and practical 220 rounds per minute was considerably better than that of the 20mm Flak 30. Yet the Flak 30 was preferred by the troops, as it was quieter and more stable when firing, thanks to its greater weight, and its somewhat lower firing speed of a magazine (= 20 rounds) in 4 seconds offered more chances to make corrections during firing. An identifying mark of the 20mm flak 38 is the circular baseplate of the cradle support on the upper mount.

For the sake of completeness it should be noted that there was also a 20mm Mountain Flak 38. Even in testing, though, it did not prove itself. The standard 20mm Flak 38 on a light special trailer for mountain forces and paratroopers also lacked accuracy because of its lack of stability. Only small numbers of them were made in 1944-45.

There were also a few 20mm Flak 38 twins. They were generally built in permanently in this form, for example, on ships, boats, ferries and railroad cars.

Above: 20mm Flak 38 on Special Trailer 51 with Flak Sight 35, seen from right rear.

Right: 20mm Flak 38 ready to travel on Special Trailer 51, seen from left. The magazine table is easy to see on the left wall of the mount.

Upper left: 20mm Flak 38 in firing position, with a barrel elevation of 45 degrees. Note the round cover of the cradle support and the swinging arm with the Flak Sight 35.

Above: The K1 turns the elevation handwheel of a 20mm Flak 38 with his right hand. The Linear Sight 21 can be seen very clearly.(BA)

Left: 20mm Flak 38, here with Flak Sight 35.

Above: The K5 carries a Range Finder 1m R36 (Em 1m R36) on a shoulder carrier. The container that the K5 carries on his back holds the source of light for the range finder.(BA)

Above: Luftwaffe aides visit a 20mm Flak gun position. In the right foreground, the pivoted ring sight is easy to see.(BA)

Right: Here a "position on wheels" of a 20mm Flak 38 for use against ground targets is seen in training. In this "position on wheels" of the 38 gun, the gunner cannot aim from his seat, since it is attached on the right side of the upper mount and must be folded up in firing position. The K1 aims at the target by using the 3 x 8 ground target telescope. K1 and K3, kneeling, handle the coarse traverse aiming of the weapon on wheels. The loader, K4, is almost hidden by the gun here. The leader fires the gun by using a cord, since the K1 cannot reach the foot trigger.

Above: 20mm Flak 38 in action. While an 88mm Flak gun is moved in the background, the 20mm Flak gun secures against low-level surprise attacks.

Upper left: From a hastily assumed position, a 20mm Flak 38 secures a riverbank. The 3 x 8 ground target telescope is mounted on the sight arm next to the Flak Sight 35.(BA)

Left: The gun crew has spotted the enemy on the opposite shore (picture above). The K1 has sighted them through the ground target telescope. After the kneeling K4 has placed a 20-round magazine, from the ammunition case close at hand, on the magazine table, the K1 opens fire.(BA)

20mm Flak 38 with Shields

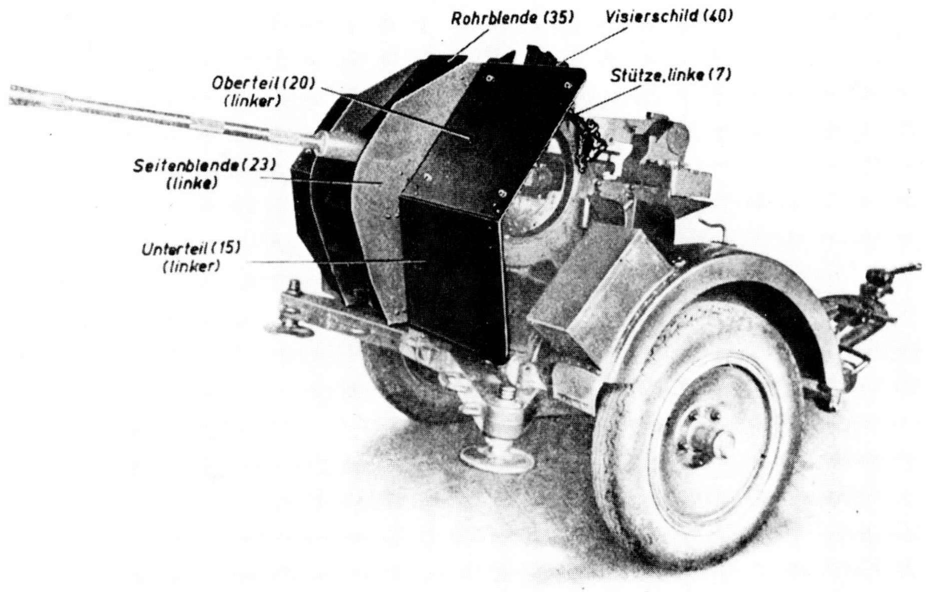

Since the 20mm Flak guns were used very often against ground targets, the guns were soon provided with shields, which made the gun 120 kg heavier.

Above: A 20mm Flak 38 with added shield for the K1, seen from ahead.

Upper right: A 20mm Flak 38 with shield, side view.

Right: A gun with shield in a prepared position in winter. Some of the crewmen wear white winter camouflage suits, which could be reversed to serve as a gray camouflage suits.(BA)

Right: From the shield of this 20mm gun before a town on the banks of the Don, the success of the crew can be seen.

This gun's special shield for the K1 is easy to see. On the sight shield hangs a pair of sun goggles for the K1. The crew's steel helmets and gas masks are beside the gun.(BA)

Upper left: The 20mm Flak proved itself on all fronts through its mobility and firepower. The gun and crew have only makeshift protection here, using canvas covers, from heat and all-pervasive dust.

Upper right: Firing drill at ground targets; steel helmets at right and ammunition cases in the foreground have been placed ready for use. The crew stands as prescribed. The leader with his binoculars is behind the K1 gunner who sits (covered) in his seat, aims at the target and triggers firing. K2 (ammunition mover) stands (also covered) behind K3 and, like him, brings up filled magazines. K4 (loader, at the gun) loads magazines and exchanges them with K3. The rangetaker in the right foreground holds the Em 1m R36 on his shoulder and takes the range.(BA)

Lower left: This only slightly camouflaged gun has been placed in position on a field. Steel helmets and gas masks with canisters are arranged handily around the gun.(BA)

Lower right: The crew of a 20mm Flak 38 and the commander of a tank tensely await the approach of enemy aircraft.(BA)

Upper left: Here a gun position is practically engulfed in mud and water during the mud season in Russia. To keep the gun ready for action, the crew forms a bucket brigade.

Above: The cartridge catcher and the armor shield for the K1 of this 20mm Flak 38 are easy to see.(BA)

Left: Here a well-camouflaged 20mm Flak 38 with armor shield is being positioned in a wheatfield. The gun is placed in position by its crew, with even the lieutenant helping out.(BA)

Above: The versatile gun was also used on ferries. Here is a flak ferry in the channel before Kertsch. Flak ferries were also used on Lake Ladoga and the Danube.

Upper right: Here a Siebel ferry is in action during the evacuation of Crimea. It carries 20mm twin and quadruple Flak guns.

Right: A 20mm Flak on a railroad car — seen on the horizon —secures a ferry slip.(BA)

The longer the war lasted, the more captured and civilian vehicles were rebuilt for the light Flak guns (here a 20mm Flak 38). Here is a very unusual example (with covered crew space!).(BA)

20mm Quadruple Flak

The 20mm Quadruple Flak 38 was adopted by the navy in 1940. Four guns were combined on one mount. With them from 800 to at most 1800 rounds per minute could be fired at a range of 4.8 km and an altitude of 3.7 km. Because of this high firepower, the gun was used very successfully not only against air targets, but also in ground combat. Therefore production was increased in 1944 from 200 to 410 per month. The Luftwaffe alone, between August 1944 and February 1945, had 3600 to 3850 units of this type.

Below: The gun crew of a 20mm Flak 38 attentively watches low-flying planes, so as to be ready to intervene at once if the ferry is attacked.(BA)

20mm Quadruple Flak, Mobile

Upper left: A 20mm Quadruple Flak 38 on Special Trailer 52 goes into position in North Africa. The crew has dismounted and lowers the gun from the trailer by using two cranks. The side pieces of the shield are still folded in.(BA)

Above: The gun is lowered and the trailer removed. With the help of three adjusting spindles on the lower mount, the gun is leveled horizontally. The side pieces of the shield have been folded out. An ammunition mover has taken three magazines from the ammunition case in the foreground.(BA)

Left: The target is spotted and aimed at by the K1. The burst of fire has raised a cloud of dust before the gun. Crew members watch to see the success of this firing.(BA)

20mm Quadruple Flak in Permanent Position

Above: The leader has ordered "Full cover!"(BA)

Right: Besides mobile 20mm quadruple Flak guns, they were also permanently placed, especially by objects that had to be protected at all times, such as cities, industrial sites, important bridges and harbors. Here a quadruple Flak 38 is mounted on a Flak tower in a big city.

Below: A barrel of the 20mm Flak 38 with muzzle brake.(BA)

A permanently placed quadruple Flak 38 beside the Oder near Küstrin, March 1945.

The spotter of a 20mm quadruple Flak gun carefully observes the air space in a flooded area in Holland.(BA)

In the west Flak guns were also used frequently at night. Upper right: The crew of a quadruple Flak gun on a Flak tower in a city. Below: Barrage fire from (mostly) 20mm quadruple Flak guns during a night attack.

20mm Flak for Railroad Protection

Flak protection always accompanied especially important rail transport, whether as single guns (left page), twins (left page, below) or quadruple guns (right).

Individually:
Far left: In general, it was customary to run a flatcar before and behind the gun car, so as to have unobstructed sight and space for firing. This was often not done for action against partisans in Russia, or on this train for furloughed front soldiers. The lower mount of this 20mm gun has only the lower circular track, by which the gun is attached to a base.(BA)

Upper left: This train carries an escort of two 20mm Flak 38 guns. To keep a safe distance between the two guns, a flatcar has been placed between them.(BA)

Lower left: A 20mm twin Flak gun on an armored railroad car.(BA)

Above: Mussolini receives two special Flak railroad cars from Germany. Each car had two quadruple 20mm Flak 38 guns, for a total firepower of 16 barrels.
Right: A 20mm quadruple Flak protects rail transport in Russia.(BA)

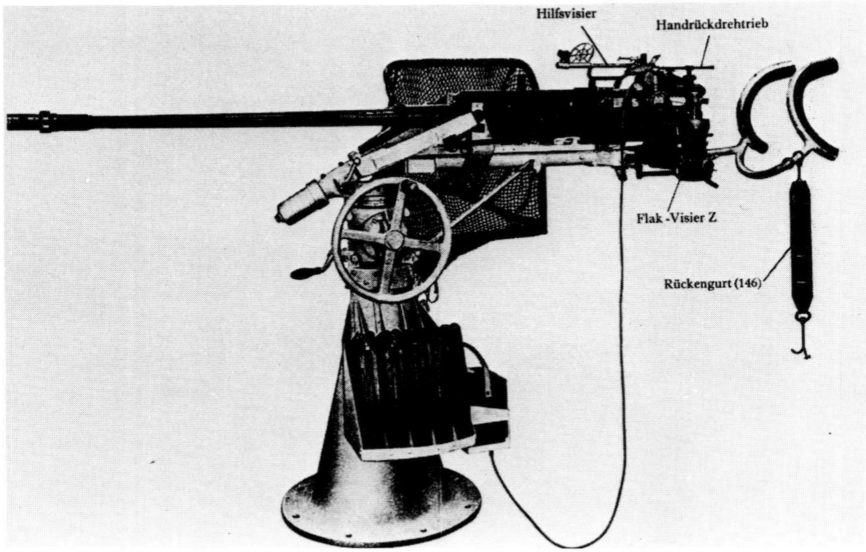

20mm Flak in the Navy

The 20mm Flak guns were used not only by the Luftwaffe and the Army, but also by the Navy. Here are two examples:
Above: The single 20mm gun on a base. The gunner aimed the gun while standing, with the help of the shoulder braces and the Flak sight. The back belt prevented him from slipping out of the shoulder braces. The holder for five magazines can be seen clearly on the base. The big cartridge catcher is also easy to see.

Right: A 20mm quad on an artillery carrier. These were ships especially equipped for anti-aircraft defense. The men wore flotation devices in combat.

In conclusion it can be said that there was no front, no ship, no fighting force and practically no service arm that did not use the 20mm Flak gun in some way. At the fronts, especially in the east, they were used more for ground combat than against aircraft.

To make them more mobile and more quickly ready to fire, these guns were soon combined with vehicles of all kinds. At first — produced by industry in peacetime — they were mounted on one-ton towing tractors, later also on auxiliary trucks and on armored vehicles, and in quadruple form.

In the following section of this volume, we shall try to cover this area — also including other Flak calibers — as completely as possible.

Self-Propelled Flak Guns

In a broad sense, we can differentiate between:
— Flak guns on wheeled vehicles,
— Flak guns on unarmored halftracks,
— Flak guns on halftracks with improvised armor,
— Flak guns on SPW halftracks,
— Flak guns on full-track vehicles, and
— Flak guns on tanks.

It is hard to decide whether Flak guns on fully tracked vehicles can all be called "Flak-panzer", or whether they should only be called tanks if they have a rotating turret closed at the top.

The following presentation is surely not complete, for the troops left practically nothing untried in terms of improvisations. Industry too was not lacking in plans that were still pending when the war ended.

Upper right: Even when fired from a sled in time of need, it cannot be called self-propelled — on account of the horses.

Right: A captured truck (Canadian CMP) carrying a 20mm Flak 30.(BA)

Flak Guns on Wheeled Vehicles

The following types are known to have existed:

— 20mm Flak 30 on Vehicle 70 (6 x 4 Krupp L2H 143), the so-called "ProtzKw", and on captured trucks,

— 20mm Flak 38, also on the ProtzKw, the heavy E-Pkw (Kfz. 69), the Horch Kübel and captured trucks, the last two only in Africa,

— 20mm quadruple Flak 38 on the partly armored Opel Blitz 3-ton truck, and

— 37mm Flak on the partly armored Mercedes-Benz L4500A and Ford 3-ton 4x2 trucks.

Left page:
Above: A 20mm Flak 38 on the reinforced platform of a (presumably captured) truck in North Africa.(BA)

Lower left: Here a Horch s.E.Pkw. Kfz. 69 is used as a gun carrier (20mm Flak 38).

Lower right: A Kfz. 70 with a 20mm Flak gun in action with the SS Panzer Division ***Wiking*** in southern Russia.

This page:
Above: A 20mm quadruple Flak gun on a 3-ton Opel Blitz truck with trailer. The cab and radiator of the truck are armored.(BA)
Upper right: A 37mm Flak gun on a partly armored Mercedes-Benz L4500A truck. There were only a few combinations of this type.
Right: A 3-ton Ford 4x2 truck with a 37mm Flak gun in Russia.

Flak Guns on Unarmored Halftracks

— 20mm Flak 30 on 1-ton (Sd.Kfz. 10.4) towing tractor,
— 20mm Flak 38 on
1-ton (Sd.Kfz. 10/5) towing tractor,
Ford "Maultier" (mule),
— 20mm quadruple Flak 38 on 8-ton (Sd.Kfz. 7/1) towing tractor,
— 37mm Flak on
5-ton (Sd.Kfz. 6.2) towing tractor, as of 1941,
8-ton (Sd.Kfz. 7/2) towing tractor, as of 1942,
— 88mm Flak on 12-ton towing tractor.

The two pictures below also show the 20mm gun on the 1-ton towing tractor; in the photo it is the Flak 30, in the drawing the 38.

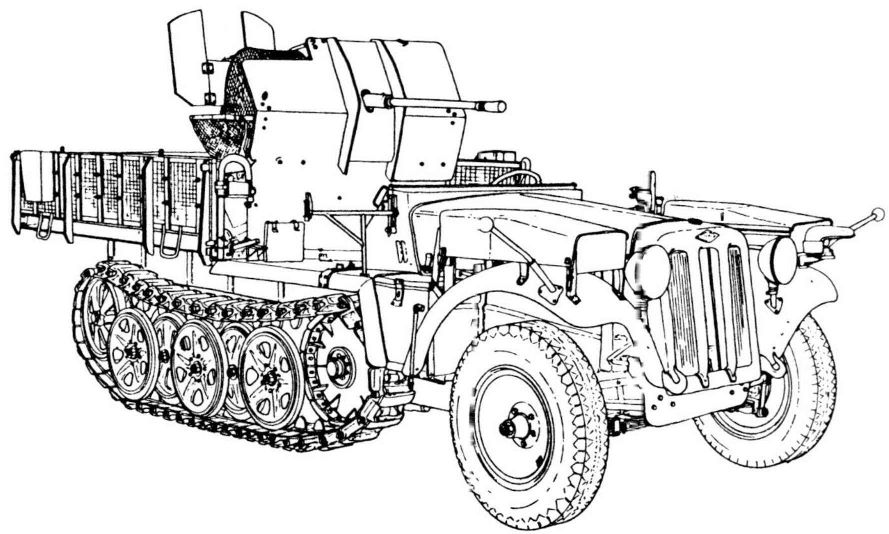

Left page, above.
A 20mm Flak 30 of the army with attached blank cartridge device, on a 1-ton towing tractor during peacetime training. The anchoring of the lower mount is easy to see, and lying in front is the rangetaker with the EM 1m R36.(BA)

On this page are three more photos of the best-known self-propelled Flak gun, the 20mm on the 1-ton towing tractor. At upper left and at right it is the Flak 30, at upper right a 20mm Flak 38.

The pictures at left each show a 20mm Flak 38 on a one-ton towing tractor. While the side panels are lowered above, they are vertical below, ready for marching. In the boxes on the front fenders are the rifles (98k carbines) of the gun crews and drivers.(BA)

In the lower picture, they are attached at the same place. Before the edge of the forest in the background stands an SPW of the engineers with assault bridges.(BA)

Above: A Ford 2-ton "Maultier" halftrack with a 20mm Flak 38 mounted on it in front of a shrapnel box.(BA)

Upper left: Two quadruple Flak guns on self-propelled mounts (8-ton towing tractors) ready to fire. Some of the crewmen wear white bandannas on account of dust.

Upper right: A gun crew during a lull in a battle. The field messenger (left) carefully observes the air space all the same. The soldiers wear field-gray combat jackets with the death's-head of the Panzer troops on the facings. These combinations did not exist until 1944.

Right: Here the shield bears camouflage paint, plus scores in the form of white stripes. The 8-ton towing tractor is called "Anny."

Flak on Halftracks with Improvised Armor

Everything is listed here that cannot be listed in the SPW category and was armored in more or less primitive form by the troops or partially, and more professionally, by the manufacturers. There were:

— 20mm Flak 30 on 1-ton towing tractors;
— 20mm Flak 38 on 1-ton towing tractors;
— 20mm quadruple Flak 38 on 8-ton towing tractors;
— 37mm Flak on
 8-ton towing tractors and
 heavy army tractors (SWS), and
— 88mm Flak on 12- or 18-ton towing tractors.

Left: A 20mm quadruple Flak on the march through Vienna.

A 37mm Flak on a 5-ton towing tractor.

A lightly armored (improvised) 1-ton towing tractor with a 20mm Flak gun and ammunition trailer.(BA)

Right: Two 8-ton towing tractors with 37mm Flak 36 guns, in front of Castello Sant'angelo in Rome.

Below and bottom right:
37mm Flak 43 on the heavy army tractor (SWS). This was built by Büssing NAG and replaced the 5-ton towing tractor. It can be recognized by its less pierced wheels. It also existed in unarmored form.

Though the armored vehicles protected the driver and passenger, the gun crew, despite the shield, was always exposed to heavy shells and shrapnel.

The famous 88mm Flak on an 18-ton towing tractor. The partial armor protects the driver, passenger and motor, but not the gun crew. The advantage of this combination was that it — like all self-propelled mounts — was that it was ready to fire more quickly than when a gun was towed. Yet in this case it took somewhat longer than with the smaller calibers because two jacks had to be put in place on each side first to absorb the recoil and the resulting bouncing of the vehicle.

Flak on the SPW

151/15 - and MG 151/20 (both aircraft weapons) in triple form (Sd.Kfz. 251/21),
20mm aircraft weapons in triple form,
20mm Flak 38
without rear armor plate (only in Africa), and
with lowering side armor, somewhat larger than the standard SPW (Sd.Kfz. 251/17).

Below: A (long) SPW with triple MG 151/15. It was also built with triple MG 151/20 — both guns used in aircraft.

Above: Here is an army Flak artillery development, presumably used only in Africa. A medium SPW with the rear armor removed carries a 20mm Flak gun, but the crew remains unprotected.

Upper left: Here triple 20mm guns are used. The SPW (Sd.Kfz. 251/21) is being shown to Hitler.

Left: This picture shows the Luftwaffe Flak artillery development (note the WL on the license plate) in comparison to the picture above. On this vehicle the side armor has been replaced by overhanging and folding armor plates. They had to be folded down for ground combat — just when the crews needed their protection. Thus this was not an ideal solution.

Flak on Full-track Vehicles

In 1941 the mountain Jäger units were supplied with combinations of the 20mm Flak 38 and Renault Chenillettes or Scout Carriers. In 1942 these guns were mounted on the reliable chassis of the 38 (t) medium tank, thus creating the first full-track Flak vehicle (Sd.Kfz. 140). The armoring of the body was like that of the SPW. The expense for just one small 20mm gun was so high, though, that requests were soon made for multipurpose weapons or larger calibers. Since the hull of the 38 (t) tank was too small, the chassis of the Panzer IV was chosen for further combinations.

A dropside platform of sheet armor with enough space for quadruple 20mm guns or a 37mm Flak 36 and their crew was first mounted on it. With the sides up, though, this was a very high vehicle easily recognized from the air. In addition, the crew had to let the sidewalls down to have full use of their weapons, which left them unprotected and made the vehicle scarcely more useful than an unarmored towing tractor — except for the driver. Because of its unusual appearance, this beast was nicknamed "Möbelwagen" (Moving Van) by the troops, and was rejected for the reasons just cited.

Experiments were also made to mount the 88mm Flak gun on armored chassis. We are not speaking here of the "Hornisse" (Hornet), later renamed "Nashorn", but of a combination that allowed the 88mm gun to be used as an anti-aircraft gun, elevated to the highest (90-degree) angle. The special chassis seen in this picture was given a body with dropping sidewalls. With the sides up, though, the gun could not be pointed forward.

Since the "Nashorn" and, above all, the "Tiger", were more useful, and since the 88 was not needed as an anti-aircraft gun on the battlefield, this vehicle too was not supplied to the troops.

Left: A 20mm Flak 38 on a British Scout Carrier. The crew sat close behind the gun; the swastika flag provided recognition from the air.(BA)

On the right page are four pictures of Sd.Kfz. 140 (20mm Flak 38 on the dependable 38 (t) chassis). In the lower left picture it can be seen that when necessary (ground combat), the upper plates of the sidewalls could be folded down.(BA)

13

13

This page and the two left pictures on the right page show the Panzer IV with quadruple 20mm Flak 38 guns behind folding armor plates. Because of its high body it was nicknamed "Möbelwagen" (Moving Van). The pictures show its varying potential: Upper left, folded down for ground combat. Upper right, folded down for anti-aircraft use. Lower left: Anti-aircraft use with angled armor walls to make room for the crew. Lower right, ready for marching, with vertical walls; right page, above, with front plate folded down.(2 x BA)

The 37mm Flak 43 (L/60) "Möbelwagen" is shown above and below. It was unusually expensive for the caliber, and thus not many were built.

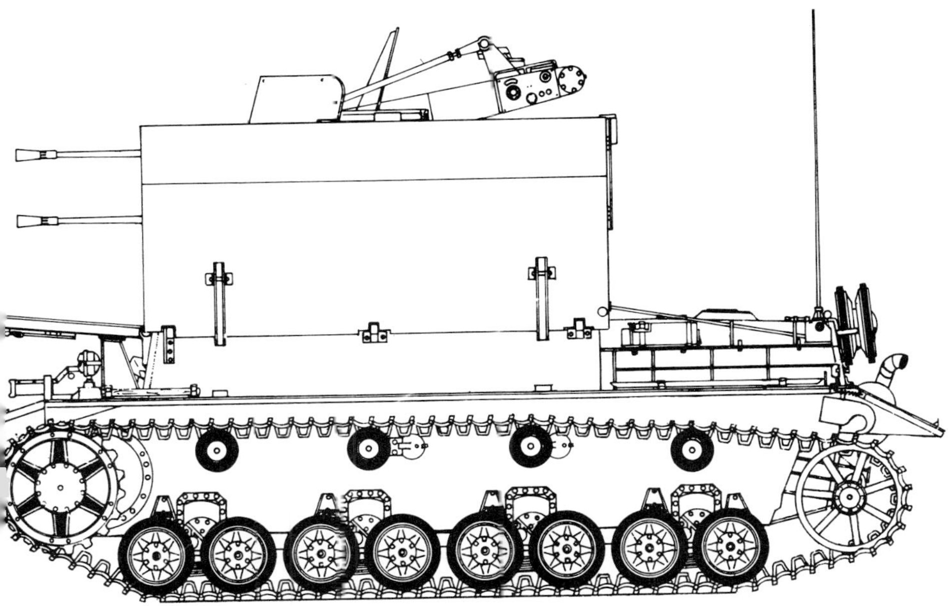

88mm Flak guns on a chassis developed for them. It could be used for anti-aircraft and ground (without folding the sides down) combat. Since the Tiger was better suited to the latter use and the 88mm Flak gun was not needed on the battlefield, it was stillborn.

Flak Tanks

If a Flak gun was to be immediately ready for action on the battlefield and fully able to follow the troops fighting in front of it, it was necessary to replace the problematic folding sides, useless in combat, with an armored rotating turret. But the necessary space for guns and crews and the shot-deflecting shapes of the armor plate resulted in rather large round turrets. In addition, the first turrets were always open at the top. Yet these versions, named "Wirbelwind" (Whirlwind) with quadruple 20mm Flak 38 guns and "Ostwind" (East Wind) with the 37mm Flak 36, proved to be successful. The rotating turret was a big step forward in the direction of Flak tanks.

The first real Flak tank, though, was built only at the end of the war and named "Kugelblitz" (Ball Lightning). It was armed with triple 30mm MK 103 aircraft guns, since the standard Flak weapons were too big to fit into a closed turret. Yet only two prototypes of this vehicle were made, and they never reached the troops.

Since the Panzer IV chassis proved to be too expensive for two 30mm guns, Daimler-Benz developed a "Small Kugelblitz" on the 38 (t) tank chassis, armed with both this and (!) twin 20mm 151/20 aircraft guns linked to it.

The Alkett firm developed a "Destroyer 45" that consisted of a Panzer VI chassis and quadruple 30mm MK 103/38 or twin 37mm Flak 43 guns. Beyond that, the Ostbau firm worked on a "Wirbelwind II" with twin 37mm Flak 44 guns. All of these developments never got beyond the drawing board or the prototype stage before the war ended.

Below: The only genuine Flak tanks that reached the troops were the "Wirbelwind" and "Ostwind." At lower left is a "Wirbelwind" (rotating turret with quadruple 20mm Flak 38 on Panzer VI chassis), at lower right the same type, abandoned by German troops and photographed by Allied soldiers.

American soldiers near Houffalize, Belgium, examine two "Wirbelwind" captured during the battle of the Ardennes in the winter of 1944-45. At upper right, two well-camouflaged "Wirbelwind" are seen on the march.

Right: The 37mm "Ostwind" Flak tank.

Below: In the foreground is a 37mm "Ostwind" Flak tank, in the background a "Wirbelwind."

Lower right: The "Kugelblitz" prototype, the first Flak tank with a closed turret. It was armed with two 30mm MK 103 aircraft guns. It never reached the troops.

In Retrospect

In conclusion, it can be said that, aside from the "Kugelblitz", no true Flak tank was used by Germany in the war, but that usable makeshift vehicles were made, and there was no lack of further ideas when the war ended.

Flak on the battlefield had only the task of protecting its own troops against low-flying (pursuit or dive bomber) enemy planes. Since it could do that only when accompanying its own battle groups, motorization and armor were necessary. For the latter, though, protection against light weapons and shrapnel was sufficient. On the other hand, the 20 to 40mm caliber guns were equal to these tasks. To avoid creating a "Möbelwagen", though, a Flak gun was needed with smaller dimensions (more automatic functions, divided mounts) than the available anti-aircraft guns of the time had. For understandable reasons, the development of the aircraft weapons was another reason why they were used so often in the last years of the war.

The ideal Flak tank would have been a lightly armored vehicle with multiple 20 or 37mm guns of compact dimensions. All other combinations, like the use of battle tank chassis and large-caliber guns, were mistakes. In part, though, they were built because Flak guns were often used on the battlefield against enemy ground targets, and thus they had to take on — usually out of necessity — tasks of the battle tanks and, above all, the tank destroyers.